BRUCE LEE, October 1962
From Mr. DeMile's personal collection.

TRIPLE YOUR STRIKING POWER

BRUCE LEE'S 1 and 3 Inch
Power Punch

by James W. DeMile

ACKNOWLEDGEMENTS

Sincere thanks to Rodney "Kimo" Wong, Ed Lobley, Rick Caudle, Richard Crandall and Mark Fineman for their help in demonstrating the techniques. Thanks also to my colleague, Dr. L.V. Biffer, for his interest and help in writing this book, and a special thanks to Steve Friend for photography.

TAO OF WING CHUN DO
2912C So. Skagit Highway
Sedro Woolley, WA 98284

ISBN 0-918642-02-7

Contents

Cautions
to be Observed

When practicing the Floating Punch, never strike a person directly. Always place something firm (such as a large phone book) between you and the point you are going to strike.

This punch immobilizes your opponent with a single strike. It is a deadly punch. Never use it in sparring matches. If the jaw is hit, the cerebral cortex will shift in its fluid with tremendous impact, knocking out your opponent and, because of the shock, possibly causing brain damage. Also the snapping action of the head may break the neck. If the area of the solar plexus is hit, the lungs will collapse with possible internal hemorrhaging. If the heart is hit, the heart valves may be broken, causing instant death. If the kidneys are hit, the kidney function may be destroyed.

Only when absolute confidence and control of this punch are attained can you actually strike an individual without protection in between. Then use only a small portion of your striking power in order to show the effectiveness of this blow. Usually when I strike in demonstrations, I strike to the left of the heart in the general area of the solar plexus so that the individual can feel his lungs collapse slightly. Never demonstrate this technique on anyone with any type of lung or heart problem.

Introduction

To my knowledge, I am one of the few people to whom Bruce Lee ever taught the Power Punch, not because it is difficult to do, but simply because Bruce wanted to keep it an exclusive technique. Although I agreed with him at the time, I now feel that the techniques should be taught to all those who wish to develop their striking power without having to dedicate themselves to the martial arts.

It is my contention that although the Power Punch, also referred to as the Floating Punch, fits in well and complements a student of the martial arts, it can be learned and executed by the average individual wanting only to effectively strike an opponent if it should become necessary. My experiences have shown me that in any physical encounter it is more often how well you can strike rather than how many martial arts techniques you know that will determine the winner.

I am not showing this technique to shortcut what a person may need for self defense; I am simply offering it as a primary tool to help the individual gain confidence in his personal capabilities.

Please read carefully all the instructions and understand the principles of each move before going on to the next step. Your success or failure in learning this strike will depend not only on how well you can do the physical and mental exercises, but on how well you understand the over-all principles that make this a dynamic and unique technique.

Although I feel this manual includes sufficient information for a reader to become proficient at the Power Punch, if any questions arise after reading and trying the techniques enclosed, please send your questions and a self-addressed, stamped envelope to:

James W. DeMile
2912-C So. Skagit Highway
Sedro Woolley, WA 98284.

Mind Development

Although the mental development is much shorter than the physical, it is of equal importance since the Floating Punch is the unification of both mental and physical strengths. The mental is in two parts — the control and direction of your thoughts, and the control and direction of your breathing, a mental process.

1. CONTROL AND DIRECTION OF YOUR THOUGHTS

In order to establish the maximum use of your potential in effectively striking a specific point, you must condition the mind to clear itself and the body of all unnecessary distractions. You must do this early in your program so that later on it will become second nature.

Letting Down Exercise — Isolate yourself so that you will not be disturbed for at least 15 minutes. There should be darkness or subdued lighting. Loosen any tight clothing and just relax.

Sit or lie in a comfortable position so that there is equal pressure throughout the body. Close your eyes. Imagine that you are looking out into space; there are no stars or lights, just total emptiness. Once you can see this emptiness clearly, take a deep breath and as you exhale, imagine yourself stepping through the doorway of your mind into that emptiness — just floating, free of all your worldly problems and tensions.

As you are drifting, first think of relaxing each segment of your body. Start with the head, imagining all the facial muscles just relaxing. Let the forehead, cheeks and jaw muscles become loose and limp. Then move down into the neck, back, shoulders, arms, hands and the rest of the body. Keep your eyes closed and stay adrift in the mental void at all times. Once you feel really relaxed, begin to think to yourself the following suggestions: "I am completely relaxing every muscle, every nerve, every fiber in my body. As I relax, I will have no outside disturbances or distractions. I will free myself from both mental and physical tension, allowing myself to feel a warm, comfortable, light feeling, like floating. My mind is going to become very sensitive to the pleasant and tranquil feeling of drifting, so that no matter where I am or how I feel, I will clear my mind of all disturbances and distractions and be able to focus on a specific desired point when I say the word 'relax'."

These above suggestions may be changed to fit your own words, or you may imagine anything you like that will establish a warm, drifting, comfortable feeling. With very little practice you will actually react to your keyword of 'relax'. By relaxing at a moments notice in tense situations, with very little effort you will mentally be able to channel your energies to a specific point.

Once you can accomplish a smooth, relaxed feeling by using your keyword, then try it in different situations — at work or social events, while standing or sitting, with eyes closed or open. Quickly you will learn to relax no matter where you are or how you feel. Master this before you proceed, since this control and direction of your thoughts will set the base for the mental-physical aspects of the Floating Punch.

2. CONTROL AND DIRECTION OF YOUR BREATHING

For a moment, let's consider your physical muscular power like an electrical energy vibrating and flowing throughout the body. This energy will fill every part of your body. It is important that you spend a little bit of time just imagining this energy being like a fluid which you can actually feel.

Once you have done this, change your attention to your breathing. Close your eyes. Draw in a slow, deep breath through your nose. Imagine your breath a dynamic and explosive life force, being drawn not only into the lungs but completely throughout the body. This causes you to feel a building of strength throughout the whole body so that by the time you have filled your lungs to capacity, you will have a powerful explosive feeling throughout. Then, as you exhale, just imagine this life force being slowly pushed out through pursed lips, draining your body of this dynamic life force, leaving you with an empty hollow feeling. Then repeat the process.

Once you feel comfortable with this technique and can do it easily, begin to focus the breath into certain parts of the body, trying to place all that dynamic energy into that area, leaving the rest of the body hollow and empty. After developing this step, use the same technique but taking in a little less air and then holding it as long as you can. While holding it, imagine that life force moving from one part of the body to another.

As an example, as you breathe in, imagine all energy is going down into the left leg so that you are distinctly aware of your left leg feeling full, and different from the rest of the body. Then while holding your breath, imagine it flowing around into the right leg so that when the right leg is full and complete, the left leg feels hollow and empty. Then, if you can still hold your breath, imagine it moving up into your right arm leaving the right leg hollow and empty and the right arm with a full feeling.

Become proficient at these steps. Then as you exhale, begin to imagine the energy flowing, not only out of your pursed lips, but rushing down your arm and out your striking fist.

Physical Development

PRIMARY AREAS OF DEVELOPMENT

The intensity of the Floating Punch is determined by the joint effort of the mind and body coordinating the movement. The power of the punch can be increased by developing certain primary areas of the body. These primary areas are the wrist, hand, elbow tendons, the triceps, and the shoulder and upper back muscles. With the proper body coordination, these primary areas of strength will be channelled into one focused point of delivery.

WRIST ROLL

Exercise for the Wrists and Shoulders.

Equipment Needed: Two 5 pound weights attached to a handle by a rope or cord. The length of the cord should be such that when you are in the proper beginning position, the weight will barely be off the floor.

Stand against a wall so that your head, buttocks and heels are flat against it. Hold the handle at each end so that you have a firm grip and there is enough room in the center of the handle to wind up all the cord without interfering with your hand movement. The weight should be 2 to 3 inches from the floor.

Raise your arms in front of you with the elbows locked and the palms facing down. Through this whole exercise your hands stay in the area between your ears and your shoulders, no higher or lower. *Do not bend the elbows at any time.* Keep your head, buttocks and heels against the wall.

Position the cord so that it is on the inside of the handle (closest to you). Without moving your arms, steadily wind the cord on the handle, using only wrist action. *Both hands* must equally raise the weight. Roll up the cord until the weight touches your hands. Then lower it until it is 2 or 3 inches from the floor. This exercise should be done initially for at least one minute each time. You should not stop moving the weight during this minute.

This exercise may also be done away from the wall. Stand vertical with the feet parallel and a little less than shoulder width apart.

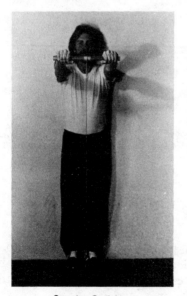

Starting Position

Raised Position

TIGER PUSHUPS

Exercise for strengthening the wrist, elbow, biceps, triceps, shoulder and back muscles.

Kneel with feet flat against the wall. Place your hands palm down and turned inward so the fingertips touch. The hands should be directly below your mouth as if you were looking down at them.

Starting Position

Now raise your body until your arms and legs are straight, with the elbows and knees locked.

Raised Position

Without bending your knees, allow your elbows to bend, dropping your body down until your forehead touches your hands. Then return to your resting position. Do this for 1 minute without resting.

Lowered Position

HAND GRIPS
Exercise for the hand, wrist and forearm muscles.

Equipment Needed: A pair of athletic hand grips and a watch or clock with a second sweep hand.

Hold the hand spring as shown in the picture. Place a watch or clock so that you can see the movement of the second hand. Start from an open position. Squeeze the springs closed and open as fast as you can, for 15 seconds. Then hold them closed as tight as you can for 15 seconds. Then squeeze them closed and open for another 15 seconds and then hold them closed again for 15 seconds. Repeat this sequence for 1 minute.

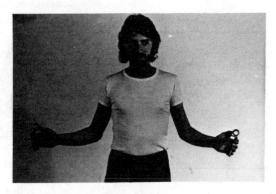

Ready Position

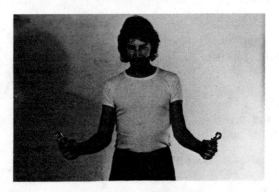

Closed Position

ISOMETRICS

Exercise for elbow tendons, triceps, biceps, shoulder and upper back muscles.

Body Position

Stand where you are able to push or lift at a point similar to the picture. Place one foot in front of the other about 2 feet apart. Close your hands into fists and place both wrists vertically under the isometric bar. Start with your elbows next to your body. Lift with all your strength for 6 seconds. Then move your body back a few inches and do it again. Move a few more inches back and repeat. Do this until you can go back no farther; then do it returning to your starting point. As you move backward and forward, push upward and forward toward the starting position

Wrist Position

Overview
of Chapters 3 & 4

The first segment of this manual has dealt with the development of your mind and your body. The next chapters will first of all explain the ready stances; secondly, devote time to the coordination exercises necessary to develop the proper knee, shoulder and arm actions for the punch and last of all teach the applied move of the Floating Punch.

The term 'floating' is used when referring to this punch since until just prior to the strike, the hand and wrist are relaxed, giving the feeling of your hand floating. The Floating Punch is an internal punch since its action causes the blow to penetrate inward causing internal damage.

The basic stance for the 3 inch Floating Punch allows for the strike to be developed from what would be a very comfortable distance from your opponent. This gives you a chance to use more body torquing action with less effort. The 1 inch Floating Punch is done while standing very close to your opponent, It calls for you to condense your energy very quickly over a shorter distance, yet it delivers a tremendous amount of power.

When practicing these basic stances and coordination exercises, keep in mind that the strength of the punch is less important than your feeling a natural and flowing action. The success of your applied Floating Punch depends greatly on the strength you are able to generate as a result of your exercises.

When practicing the paper hanging exercises, do not use the Floating Punch. These exercises help you gain smoothness and control as well as speed and timing. Although you can use full intensity, never hit past the real striking point, which is the surface of the paper.

Once you are confident in your Floating Punch coordination, you may start to generate power by using the coffee can exercise. Use more power as you feel more efficient, and also begin to use your imaginary striking point to develop penetration.

The heavy bag exercises allow you to feel your blow exploding as it penetrates to your imaginary striking point. When working on anything heavy, first of all, use only the Floating Punch from the 1 and 3 inch positions so you can develop the proper timing for the wrist and fist. Once you have perfected these short range punches, try the long range Floating Punch. CAUTION: If your timing is even slightly off, you can easily break your wrist because of the greater power of the long range punch.

Once you have developed your coordination and are able to control your power, you are ready to practice the 1 and 3 inch punch for general demonstrations.

NOTE: All references made on the following pages are for striking with the right hand. To use the left, simply reverse the directions.

Exercises to Develop the Floating Punch

INTRODUCTION

These are basic stances to exercise the Floating Punch. Do not restrict yourself to the exact stance and body positions presented in this manual. When you become confident in your over-all ability to apply the techniques offered here, try exploding the Floating Punch from different stances. Testing your Floating Punch from different angles enables you to determine the strongest position.

Body weight and level of kinetic power play a definite part in the strength of your punch. Bruce Lee, who was 5 feet 7 inches tall and weighed 135 pounds, always led with his right leg. It was the only way he could explode his energy forward, into a much bigger opponent, without recoiling under his own power. Placing his strong side forward created a power base to push off, which allowed him to follow through after his blow. This follow-through pushed his opponent back after the blow had broken the opponent's balance.

Right Lead Overextended

The method just described was used by Bruce Lee in his demonstrations and is referred to as a push punch. The opponent's reaction is shock from the blow and imbalance from the push. The main disadvantage in using the push punch is the tendency to overextend your energy towards the opponent. This opens you to counterattack.

The Floating Punch should only move a few inches past the point of contact. When the opponent is pushed, much of the energy transfer is lost. This reduces the shock of the blow. If the Floating Punch is properly done, the opponent will drop where he stands rather than fly backward.

Unless used for demonstrations, all techniques explained in this manual will drop the opponent with a short exploding Floating Punch. To minimize the tendency to overextend your energy, this manual emphasizes the right foot in a rear position.

Three Inch Punch Ready Stance

Face your opponent, about 1½ feet away. Stand so that your right shoulder is in a direct line with your striking point. Your right foot can be anywhere from 5 to 10 inches back of your left foot. Toes of both feet should be pointed about 10 degrees outward. Feet should be slightly less than shoulder width apart. Hands are loose and relaxed at your sides.

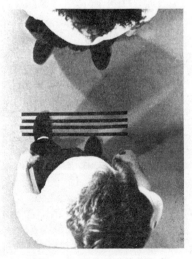

3 Inch Ready Stance — Sideview   Notice Right Foot Position

One Inch Punch Ready Stance

The ready stance for the one inch punch is the same as that for the three inch punch except the right foot is only 3 inches back of your left foot.

1 Inch Ready Stance — Sideview   Notice Right Foot Position

COORDINATION EXERCISES USING THE KNEE

These are taught to create spring load for the Floating Punch.

The Three Inch Punch Coordination Exercise Using the Knee

Firm Foot — The firm-footed position is usually used by a bulky or heavy-framed individual.

From the three inch punch ready stance, allow both knees to suddenly collapse. (You should have a momentary feeling of falling.) Your right knee moves about 3 inches towards your opponent. It creates a slight body twisting effect, and drops slightly lower than your left knee. Your left knee angles slightly outward. Your whole body drops about 3 to 6 inches and locks into position. Your right shoulder moves slightly forward and lower than your left shoulder. At this time your hands remain relaxed in the move so that you can be more aware of knee and body motion. Your feet remain flat on the floor throughout this exercise.

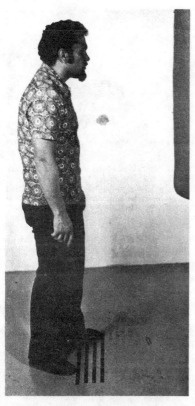

Basic 3 Inch Ready
Position for Firm Foot

3 Inch Firm Foot Position

Raised Heel — This position may be used by a heavy person, but usually lighter-framed individuals use it since it allows for more body power to be generated. (Bruce Lee used a raised heel position.) It must be practiced more carefully than the firm foot stance since finer coordination is needed.

From the three inch ready stance, allow both knees to suddenly collapse. (You should have a momentary feeling of falling.) At the same time, raise your right heel and push slightly forward off your right toes. The body and the right shoulder drop similar to the firm foot exercise, only the shoulder and knee move a little farther forward creating a torquing action. This forward move is the result of the heel raising. At this time, your hands remain relaxed in the move, so that you can be more aware of knee and body action. This movement should take only a split second.

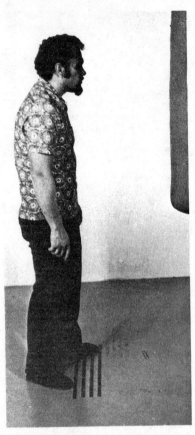 

Basic 3 Inch Ready
Position for Raised Heel

3 Inch Raised Heel Position

The One Inch Punch Coordination Exercise Using the Knee

Firm Foot — Assume the one inch punch ready stance. Follow the directions for the three inch punch firm foot knee coordination exercise, but drop down a little straighter and go forward less.

Baisc 1 Inch Ready
Position for Firm Foot

1 Inch Firm Foot Position

Raised Heel — Assume the one inch punch ready stance. Follow the directions for the three inch punch raised heel knee coordination exercise, but drop down a little straighter and go forward less.

Basic 1 Inch Ready
Position for Raised Heel

1 Inch Raised Heel Position

COORDINATION EXERCISES USING THE HANDS

These are to be done against a bag or striking pad. When striking your target, hit it only on the surface with a glancing blow. Use a vertical fist and make your hand recoil about 6 inches. Practice this for general coordination, to develop the snap for the Floating Punch, and to refine your timing and judgment. CAUTION: Strike your target only with a full vertical strike. Do not attempt to use the Floating Punch at this time since you may break your wrist.

Three Inch Punch Coordination Exercise Using the Hands

Assume a three inch ready stance about a foot and a half away from your target.

Firm Foot — As the knee begins to drop, the hand should begin its move towards the target, still relaxed. The hand clenches into a tight vertical fist a split second before the body recovers from the falling sensation caused by the knee action. The hand strikes the target, recoiling or snapping almost instantly back about 6 inches. The over-all feeling when doing this spring exercise is similar to the feeling gotten

Approach Position   Striking Position

when suddenly being startled by a touch or a sound which causes the body to jerk and tighten and then relax.

You have 2 options. 1. Draw your left hand up your left front side, palm toward your body. It comes to rest to the left of your solar plexus with the elbow lightly into the body. 2. Bring your hand directly upward and at the same time draw your elbow back around the body as far as it will go. It reaches its maximum point at the moment the right hand is striking. Both hands are coordinated so that the movement should feel balanced.

Raised Heel — Assume the ready stance as in the Firm Foot Hand Coordination Exercise. The snapping and coordination of the hand along with the knee and heel motion will be the same as in the hand exercise using the Firm Foot. The only difference is the right shoulder moves a little more forward as the right leg pushes it behind the punch. This causes more over-all body motion in the strike.

Approach Position   Striking Position

One Inch Punch Coordination Exercise Using the Hands

Stand about one foot away from your target.

Firm Foot — Keep your hands by your sides. Since you are closer to your opponent than in the three inch punch, you must drop your body down and torque your shoulder forward a little more. Also, the movement will be quicker because there is less room to move. Otherwise, the move will have the same general feeling as in the three inch hand coordination exercise.

Approach Position

Striking Position

Raised Heel — Again, since this is done in a closer area, there is a much quicker action. There is also a little deeper penetration of the striking point, almost like a push. The pushing effect lasts only a split second. Then the heel raises and the wrist and the fist snap into the punch.

Approach Position   Striking Position

PAPER STRIKING EXERCISE
Purpose: To refine the control of body coordination, timing, speed, distance and the placement of striking power.

CAUTION: This technique calls for a great degree of skill. Do not practice it unless you can concentrate and thus minimize your chances of injury. You may break your hand. Use only a vertical snapping (recoiling) strike. Do not use the Floating Punch.

Hang a piece of paper 3 inches from the wall. As you improve, move it in ½ inch moves, until the paper is flat against the wall.

Stand in your basic Floating Punch stance with your hands by your sides. Clear your mind. Take a deep breath and use your keyword, 'relax'. When you feel energy flowing throughout your body, begin. Without any sign of movement, as quickly as you can, drop the knee and strike the center of the paper with a full vertical strike of full intensity. Hit the surface so that it barely moves. After you have developed control in this basic exercise, walk briefly away from the

27

target. When you return to it, do not stand in the same spot or use the basic ready stance. Stand in an open, relaxed position and practice again. Then move between each strike always trying to hit the same spot on the paper and still barely moving it. Once you feel comfortable and confident, move the paper toward the wall ½ inch and repeat the exercise. You may move the paper until it touches the wall. When you can strike the paper on the wall at full speed and intensity without hurting your hand, you are ready to hit an opponent without using a protective device for your opponent.

On Wall Starting Position   Wall Surface Striking Position

IMAGINARY AND REAL STRIKING POINTS

Since the Floating Punch is an internal strike, your imaginary target must be at least 2 inches deeper than your real impact point. As you improve, you can vary the depth, putting two people in tandem and imagining that you are hitting the second man. (Remember to use a heavy book or object between you and your real striking point.) The hitting force is a driving energy that focuses on your inner imaginary striking point beneath the surface of real impact point. Therefore you do not need to condense your energy until a split second prior to impact. The explosive force is centered on your imaginary striking point and not wasted on external driving force. If you focus your energy too soon, it will spread out at the surface and lose its internal intensity.

Since the Floating Punch causes a sudden surge of energy into the imaginary target and all the force explodes within, it may cause internal damage. This technique enabled the masters of the martial arts to kill their opponents instantly or within a specified period without leaving a surface mark. They understood the body harmony and knew when to hit a certain area in order to cause a chain reaction of destruction that would end in death.

Imaginary and Real Striking Points

The Floating Punch

Any Floating Punch at a range of greater than 5 inches is considered a long range Floating Punch. Be very careful when using a long range Floating Punch. There is a greater need for more exact timing and coordination. The advantage of the long range Floating Punch is that you can be in a more relaxed starting position and have more over-all flexibility and generate more power.

The long range coordination exercises you have learned prepare you for both the 1 and 3 inch punches as well as the long range punch.

In the following applications of the Floating Punch, the coffee can exercise develops the snapping action of the 1 and 3 inch punch. The four movements of the Floating Punch are for the long range Floating Punch. The heavy bag techniques may be practiced first with the 1 and 3 inch punch and then the long range Floating Punch. The demonstration tips are only for the 1 and 3 inch punch.

APPLICATION OF THE FLOATING PUNCH

The body coordination, the intensity and the mental focus are for one purpose — to get the maximum amount of energy into your target. The body and the mind condense this explosive force so that the wrist and the fist can deliver it. Follow these instructions carefully or you may harm your wrist, and thus never be able to do the Floating Punch again since a weak wrist will break under its own force.

Take a three pound coffee can. Fill it with sand and tape the lid on tightly. Wrap the can with firm padding so that your hand will be protected, yet little or none of the power will be lost. Find a smooth flat surface such as a table. Raise the table so that the can is straight out from your floating rib. Place the can on the edge of the table closest to you. You will use either the 1 inch or 3 inch punch to strike the can, knocking it across the table. Since the 3 inch punch is easier, we will begin with that.

Three Inch Punch

Stand with your hands hanging loosely at your sides in your basic three inch ready stance. Keep your elbow by your side, raise your forearm and hand until they are straight out, with your extended fingers touching the can. Your hand should be open, loose and relaxed with the palm facing inward, just as in the picture.

3 Inch Ready Position

Do this slowly at first to get the feeling of it. Without raising the hand or tensing up, move the hand toward the can, at the same time closing into a loose fist. Just as the upper knuckles of the hand touch the can, suddenly close the hand into a tight fist and thrust the lower part of the fist forward (wrist twists) striking the can and at the same time firming up the whole body. The upper knuckles should hardly touch the can; in fact, they should pull away slightly as the lower knuckles strike an imaginary point inside the can. Hooking the lower knuckles upward at the moment of impact creates an arcing effect to the energy as it penetrates the opponent. This creates an internal shock effect. Do not *push* the can. From the original position (the extended

31

fingers touching the can) to impact, your fist should not have to move more than 4 inches.

If you practice this a few minutes a day, in a short time you should be able to move the can 3 to 4 feet. Of course you will have to focus and add speed and body movement in order to develop your full potential. If initially the can is too heavy, persist. Your distance will increase with practice.

One Inch Punch

The one inch Floating Punch is more difficult because you have very little room to generate power.

Stand in a 1 inch ready stance with your hands loosely by your sides. Keep your elbow by your side. Close your hand into a loose fist. Place the upper knuckles lightly against your target with your lower knuckles slightly back.

1 Inch Ready Position

The strike begins with a very slight forward motion of the upper knuckles. Without waiting for the upper knuckles to strike firmly, the lower knuckles spring forward with the body condensing down and focusing the energy transfer as quickly as possible.

Hand Position After Strike

THE FOUR MOVEMENTS
OF THE LONG-RANGE FLOATING PUNCH

When doing the Floating Punch, all movements of the body are brought together into one single action, in this simple step by step process.

1. Stand in your basic ready stance. Hands are loose and limp at your sides. Take a deep breath. Exhale. Use your key-word, 'relax'. Clear your mind of all disturbances and distractions, and just focus your attention on what you are about to do. Feel your breath like a dynamic energy, flowing totally throughout the body, getting ready, in a hundredth of a second, to flow out the striking hand.

2. In a loose, relaxed manner, the knees collapse, the body drops, the right arm fires loose and relaxed towards its target. At the exact moment of impact, the whole body becomes locked into a single unit, driving inward about 2 inches.

1

2

3. At the moment of impact, the hand, which was hanging loosely and slightly downward, clenches into a fist and (without the wrist changing its position), moves upward with the top part of the hand drawing back, striking with the lower 2 knuckles.

4. The tremendous intensity of this dynamic force should last only a split second. Then the striking hand recoils 3 to 6 inches.

3

4

If the blow is done properly, even though you are hitting through a thick book in the solar plexus area, the individual should feel his lungs reacting to the blow. You cannot be sure of the effect of the punch against a bag or post since this is an internal punch. It is only by hitting an individual, lightly at first through a thick book, and determining his physical reaction to the punch that you will be able to rate the success of your delivery of the Floating Punch technique.

These steps develop the over-all applied movement. The exercise of application is usually done practicing for the 1 or 3 inch punch against the coffee can. This minimizes injury to the wrist and develops the proper wrist and hand snapping action. As your skill develops, the punch can be done from a greater distance and with more intensity.

HEAVY BAG TECHNIQUES

The bag must be very firm without any bumps.

First, practice only your knee and hand coordination exercises. Strike the bag only on the surface and only with a vertical fist. Practicing this will help you feel more comfortable and confident in your over-all movement.

Once you have developed your Floating Punch and strengthened your wrist, you can start hitting the heavy bag with the Floating Punch and with full intensity, not only from the basic positions but from different angles and distances. Although the over-all action will be a little different because of these odd positions, you should still feel the same basic coordinated movement and snapping explosive force.

Vary the depth of your imaginary striking points and concentrate on your relaxation and breathing, along with the body coordination.

Side

Hips

DEMONSTRATION TIPS

When demonstrating the Floating Punch, never strike a person directly. Always place something firm (such as a *large* phone book) between you and the point you are going to strike. Usually for demonstrations, I strike to the left of the heart in the general area of the solar plexus so that the individual can feel his lungs collapse slightly. Never demonstrate this technique on anyone with any type of lung or heart problem.

For demonstration purposes, use only the 1 and 3 inch punch, not the long range punch. It is extremely easy to break your wrist if you hit from a distance of more than five inches since that extra distance allows you to generate more power. (In a fighting situation, you do not limit yourself to a 1 or 3 inch punch or to a basic stance; once within proper distance you can strike from any angle or distance.)

Use the 1 inch punch against one individual; never demonstrate it against two or three people. It is too easy to hurt the first person because of the need for exploding so much power.

When demonstrating the 3 inch punch, use three individuals; the second and third individuals hold firmly to the first person. They are not to push forward as this could cause the first person to absorb most of the shock.

Position of Book

Angles of Striking for Demonstration Purpose

Always allow your strike to follow a line that attacks your opponent's weakest point of balance. For example, in the pictures, strike in the angle of the line indicated. Adjust your body position to compensate for the opponent's stance so you can hit at the proper angle. If possible, develop the use of the Floating Punch with either hand so you can attack the opponent's weakest angle without having to shift your body position.

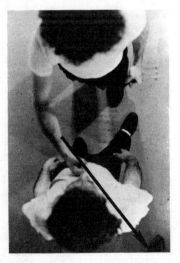

Striking Angles